Sorting Facts;
or, Nineteen Ways of
Looking at Marker

NEW DIRECTIONS POETRY PAMPHLETS

Sorting Facts;
or, Nineteen Ways of
Looking at Marker

Susan Howe

New Directions Poetry Pamphlet #1

An earlier version of this essay was first published in *Beyond Document: Essays on Nonfiction Film*, edited by Charles Warren (Wesleyan University Press, 1996).

La Jetée, by Chris Marker © 1963 Argos Films

Cover design by Office of Paul Sahre
Interior design by Eileen Baumgartner and Erik Rieselbach
Manufactured in the United States of America
New Directions Books are printed on acid-free paper.
First published as New Directions Poetry Pamphlet #1 in 2013

Library of Congress Cataloging-in-Publication Data
Howe, Susan, 1937–
Sorting facts; or, Nineteen ways of looking at Chris Marker / Susan Howe.
pages cm. — (A New Directions poetry pamphlet; no. 1)
ISBN 978-0-8112-2039-2 (paperbook: alk. paper)
1. Marker, Chris, 1921–2012 — Poetry. I. Title. II. Title: Sorting facts.
III. Title: Nineteen ways of looking at Chris Marker.
PS3558.O893S67 2013
811'.54—dc23

2012042810

10 9 8 7 6 5 4 3

New Directions Books are published for James Laughlin
by New Directions Publishing Corporation
80 Eighth Avenue, New York, NY 10011

· the FACTORY OF FACTS.

· Filming facts. Sorting facts. Disseminating facts. Agitating
with facts. Propaganda with Facts. Fists made of facts.

· Lightning flashes of facts.

· Mountains of facts.

· Hurricanes of facts.

· And individual little factlets.

· Against film-sorcery.

· Against film-mystification.

· For the genuine cinematification of the worker-peasant.
USSR.

—Dziga Vertov, 1926

I

I was originally asked to contribute an essay for a collection
called *Beyond Document: Essays on Nonfiction Film,* edited by
Charles Warren, with an Introduction by Stanley Cavell, be-
cause of a book I once wrote about Emily Dickinson's poetry.
Although this seemed a strange reason to assume I could write
about nonfiction film, I was drawn to the project because of the
fact of my husband's death and my wish to find a way to docu-
ment his life and work.

David von Schlegell was a second-generation American
with a German name. He was born in St. Louis in 1920. His
German name embarrassed him, especially the "von," but he
didn't change it, maybe because he was an only child. The family
moved east shortly after his birth when his father got a job
teaching painting at the Art Students League in New York City.
His mother's first name was Alice, but people called her Bae
(pronounced Bay). She also drew and painted. The three of
them loved the Atlantic Ocean, especially the Maine coast at

Ogunquit where they spent each summer. As a boy, David designed sailboats. When he was in his teens he built his own and called it Stormy. He hoped to become a yacht designer or an architect, but he was young and healthy enough to be cannon fodder, so from 1943 to 1945 he served as a bomber pilot and armament-systems officer in the Eighth Air Force. Until he died and was cremated he had a large scar on his left arm from where he was shot while piloting a B-17 in the fiery skies over Emden in Germany. The bullet shattered his wrist, but he managed to bring the bomber back to home base in England. Three other crew members were wounded also. It could be said this wound just above his left hand saved his life, because he was hospitalized for several months and then honorably discharged. But the war wounded him in ways he could never recover. After the war he studied painting with his father at the Art Students League. He painted for many years, then switched suddenly to sculpture. He was a shy person. His art was influenced by Russian Constructivism and various American boat designers. He worked in wood, steel, and aluminum, and usually built his own pieces. His best-known sculptures were designed in the 1960s and early 1970s. I didn't meet him until 1965 when he was forty-five and I already loved his sculpture. We lived together for twenty-seven years, most of them by Long Island Sound. Toward the end of his life he had to stop sailing because of severe arthritis in his knees, but he could still row. I liked to watch how he feathered the oars to glide back. Little whirlpools formed where the oar blades tipped under: their entry clean as their exit. These are only some facts. He had a stroke and died three days later on Monday, October 5, 1992, at 5 a.m. Those last days in the hospital were a horror. He was fully conscious, but words failed. He couldn't speak or write. He tried to communicate by gestures. We couldn't interpret them. He kept making the gesture of pointing. In physical space we couldn't see what he saw. He couldn't guide a pencil or form a coherent signal. François Truffaut says that for a filmmaker the basic problem is how to express oneself by purely visual means. The same could be said for a sculptor, except that for two days and three nights in the hospital I don't think David saw what "visual means" meant. Without words what are facts? His eyes seemed to know. His hand squeezed mine. What did he mean? In my writing, I have often explored ideas of what constitutes an official version of events as opposed to a former version in imminent danger of being lost.

Sorting word-facts I only know an apparition. Scribble grammar has no neighbor. In the name of reason I need to record something because I am a survivor in this ocean.

That's why I agreed to meddle in a foreign discipline.

It's almost next October. In Connecticut we call warm days in October Indian summer. In an interview with Phillipe Sollers, Jean-Luc Godard, referring to *Hail Mary*, cited a passage from Antonin Artaud: "I want soul to be body, so they won't be able to say that the body is soul, because it will be the soul which is body." Godard said this helped him to explain things to his film technicians.[1]

Surely nonfiction filmmakers sometimes work intuitively by factual telepathy. I call poetry *factual telepathy*.

---

1 The interview is printed in Jean-Luc Godard's "Hail Mary": *Women and the Sacred in Film*, ed. Maryel Locke and Charles Warren (Southern Illinois University Press, 1993). 123–24.

II

The French documentary filmmaker, photographer, and traveler, Chris Marker, was a poet first. Marker's twenty-eight-minute *La Jetée*, written and photographed during the early 1960s, imagines a third world war. A man, marked by an image from his childhood, travels through some intertranslational fragmented mirror-memory to the original line of fracture no translation will pacify. Many pilots, men and women, survived, though they didn't survive, collective military service during World War II. *La Jetée* (1962) and *Sans Soleil* (1982) are haunted by indwelling flames of spirit. In the beginning of each Marker film jet planes escape the eye of the camera. One is overhead roaring murder. We see the other being concealed under the flight-deck of an aircraft carrier. *La Jetée* is called a ciné-roman; *Sans Soleil* a documentary.

III

Life, Life

In 1927 one of Vladimir Mayakovsky's directives for a Constructivist Poetics of Revolution was: "Let's drop all this gibberish about unfurling 'the epic canvas' during a period of war on the barricades—your canvas will be torn to shreds on all sides."[2] Dziga Vertov certainly agreed. Both were iconoclastic image-makers, though this may be an oxymoron. Oxymorons are incongruous; they mimic and contradict. Iconoclastic image-makers and oxymorons parody habitual thought patterns while marking a site of convergence and conflict: split-repetition, acceleration, reverse motion.

"Revolutionary cinema's path of development has been found," Vertov declared boldly in 1929. "It leads past the heads of film actors and beyond the studio roof, into life, into genuine reality, full of its own drama and detective plots" (KE 32). He considered Mayakovsky's aesthetics of poetry to be closely identified with his own aspirations for radical change in film production: change that would emphasize the primacy of the "factual." The essence of fact was to be found in the poetry of reality; in material objects.

Vertov's debut in cinema prophetically involved a fall. The poet-filmmaker-documentarist ordered his cameraman to shoot him as he jumped off the roof of a one-and-a-half story summer house. The cameraman was instructed to record Vertov's leap so that all of his real thoughts while falling would be visible on film. Vertov hoped to show that while the ordinary human eye can't ever see what a person is really thinking or feeling during the immediate chaos of violent motion, the camera's

2 Quoted in *Kino-Eye: The Writings of Dziga Vertov*, ed. Annette Michelson, trans. Kevin O'Brien (University of California Press, 1984), xxvii. Further citations to this book are given with the abbreviation KE.

technical eye, oscillating between presence and absence, can frame and arrest that person with thoughts in place. Accelerated motion, recalled from a distance of constructed stillness, can recuperate the hiddenness and mystery of this "visible" world.

Is it sense perception or depiction I see "thinking"?

A still photo in *Kino-Eye: The Writings of Dziga Vertov* shows the dapper realist, non-acting, quick-change artist, wearing a white cotton shirt, sleeves folded to the elbows, a wristwatch, casual slacks, white socks, and elegant white shoes, on a day before World War II. Vertov's right hand touches the crown of his head, as if to measure his position inside the space-time of a film frame. His left arm is reaching forward, probably for balance. He is posing while falling upright and cautiously smiling. From this perspective he appears to be an enlightened materialist.

He could be thinking "I told you so," looking out.

In 1934 an older and more subdued enthusiast of realism noted in his journal: "Several years have now passed since Mayakovsky's death. In every area of our life tremendous changes have taken place. And only the script departments continue as before to defend their hackneyed principles against the incursion of poetic filmmakers. The will to produce poetic film, and particularly poetic documentary, still runs up against a wall of perplexity and indifference. It generates panic. Spreads fear" (KE 184). Recalling Mayakovsky's immense energy, and his own hunger to create, Vertov tersely wrote: "We who work in documentary poetic film are dying for work" (KE 186).

"Document [fr.LL *documentum* official paper, fr. L, lesson, example, fr. *docere* to teach + -*mentum* -ment—more at

DOCILE]" "Document verb transitive," *Webster's Third New International Dictionary* (1971):

> **doc-u-ment** 1 obs: TEACH, SCHOOL, INSTRUCT 2: to evidence by documents: furnish documentary evidence of 3: to furnish with documents 4a: to furnish (a ship) with ship's papers as required by law for the manifesting of ownership and cargo b: to annex to (a bill of exchange) the shipment documents—see DOCUMENTARY BILL 5a: to provide with factual or substantial support for statements made or a hypothesis proposed esp: to equip with exact references to authoritative supporting information b: to construct or produce (as a movie or novel) with a high proportion of details closely reproducing authentic situations or events.

Under "documentary adj." the compilers, assemblers, or typographers have set the words "FACTUAL, OBJECTIVE, REPRESENTATIONAL" in caps.

Editorial use of split sequences, "disruptive-associative montage," emphasis on the mysterious patternment and subliminal structures of images (icons), sensitivity to the sound shape (even in a silent film) of each pictured event, awareness of the time-mystery of simultaneous phenomena (co-occurrence and deployment)—I am an American poet writing in the English language. I have loved watching films all my life. I work in the poetic documentary form, but didn't realize it until I tried to find a way to write an essay about two films by Chris Marker.

On January 17, 1937, Vertov asked himself: "Is it possible that I too am acting out a role? The role of seeker after film truth? Do I truly seek truth? Perhaps this too is a mask, which I myself don't realize?" (KE 209).

IV

1941!—a hole in history
—Emmanuel Levinas

The title of *Sans Soleil* is taken from a song cycle by Mussorgsky. Towards the end of the film the narrator imagines a time traveler from the year 4001, "when the human brain has reached the era of full employment." The traveler is a third-worlder of Time. He tells us Mussorgsky's songs are still sung in the 40th century. I read once that the magic of Mussorgsky rises from a sort of catastrophe. Most of *Sans Soleil's* footage was shot in Japan during the early 1970s, but shades of the dead of Hiroshima and Nagasaki hover at the margins because what is the chaos of fire to Memory? The films of Andrei Tarkovsky are also imprinted by signal recollections of our soils and losses. *Ivan's Childhood* (1962) and *Mirror* (1974), are classified as fictional films in video-rental stores, though they incessantly and insistently document the somber confines of experience during the 1940s. In *Sculpting in Time: Reflections on the Cinema* (1986) Tarkovsky examines his position in an aesthetics of film, always wondering weaving measuring intentionalities of consciousness: problems, paradoxes, time-space, dream-time, unexpected necessity, cinematic possibility. What *is* a film, he keeps asking.

· Fact?
· Forms inside a box?

· Imprinted time?
· Time in the form of fact?
· Recorded life?
· Anonymous truth?
· The print of thought?

V
Night trains air raids fall out shelters
—Sandor Krasna, 1982.

   Sans Soleil opens with an idyllic pastoral sequence. Three children are walking along a country road in Iceland. The camera's knowing eye plucked them out of place and bygone time shortly before a volcano buried their village under ash. Through the medium of film, we watch them passing through the past again. A woman's voiceover tells us the film's editor surrounded or sheltered this particular sequence with black leader. She speaks from inside the black until the next sequence of shots, when the jet plane sinks into the hold of a destroyer or aircraft carrier.

   Bearer of lethal invisible material

   only an event or nonevent lowering along the scopic field of light or flight in a world flooded with facts.

   La Jetée, composed almost completely of photo stills, begins abruptly with a violent out-of-field-movement-sound-image, the roar of revving and hovering jet engines. Sometimes I think I hear sirens, until the whine or scream of aviation doubles and dissolves into cathedral music: voices in a choir sing passages from the *Russian Liturgy of the Good Saturday*. In northern Russia, Iceland, and other northern places, the sun never goes out of sight in summer. *La Jetée's* aborted soundtrack takeoff evokes technicist and eschatological worldviews.

Immediately time could be going either way.

Sabbath. Beginning of the world to this day. The end of darkness, even in the first of *Genesis* all will of God all sum of mortal obedience. How fearfully without transition a moving image becomes a view of things according to machine assemblage. "My films are my children." Genres and methods are means washing over the projector's original phantom photogram. Firstness can only be feeling. Vertovian theory of the interval. What if a film never reaches the screen because viewers walk away?

Return to the intrusive camera for shelter.

Marker's list of credits calls *La Jetée* a "ciné-roman," but the camera's preliminary concentration on real signal towers, real runways, real airport machinery, real modernist utilitarian airport architecture, suggests a nonfiction representation of fact: socialist realism versus documentary invention.

"Ceci est l'histoire d'un homme marqué par une image d'enfance."

Concerning a voice through air

it takes space to fold time in feeling

Often in the moving time of speech some spoken words get lost. A voiceover is omnidirectional, though we read from left to right. White intertitles form lines on the circumscribed skin of a screen. Superimposed subtitles form a third chain of translation: a foreign message from someone to someone foreign. "This is the story of a man, marked by an image from childhood." Words written in English tell me the same thing twice, though through another haunted vista and approach. In 1948, just after World War II, Laurence Olivier produced, directed, and starred in *Hamlet*. Olivier's voiceover introduction to the film was a single sentence spliced to an intertitle-quotation from one of Hamlet's soliloquies: "This is the tragedy of a man who could not make up his mind."

In act 1, scene 1, Horatio sees the ghost of Hamlet's father armed, but with the visor of his helmet up. The protagonist of *La Jetée* has been granted to watch, as a child, his own death. The unknown woman, object of his wish, subject of his gaze, sometimes calls him her "Ghost." "*Hamlet*. Farewell, dear mother. *King*. Thy loving father, Hamlet. *Hamlet*. My mother. Father and mother is man and wife, man and wife is one flesh; so my mother. Come, for England."

He loses her to look for her. Escape into air from living underwater, she could be his mother glimmering into sight

if a bird beats the air must it oh

oh must it not resound

across the moving surface of time, a dark wing the hauntedness all that is in the other stream of consciousness. "So oft it chances in particular men." Now whisper about his eyes being stone. Different visor masks. The uneasy distinction. Turned aside by a look he must go back. Her face is a prisoner of Love.

A boy and his parents have come to the main jetty at Orly, the Paris airport, on a Sunday before World War III, to watch the planes taking off. A little family stands together, facing away from the camera. It's unclear if "the child whose story we are telling" is the child who has his back to us in two still shots. The off-screen narrative voice adopts the royal we when telling the story. Image track and soundtrack don't quite connect. Did the boy at the guardrail inside the film frame become the marked man? His story will survive the madness to come because of his obsession with an image he is *bound* to remember. Who or what binds him? Something he saw on that primal Sunday he looked the other way. We see a young woman standing alone at the right corner of the jetty directly under the early morning or late-afternoon sun. There is always a time when day and night are equal. She must have turned, because in another shot we see her face. Glancing our way her expression is hard to determine. Her pensive gaze is wary tender innocent dangerous. She may be remembering beckoning staring apprehending responding reflecting or deflecting his look.

The uncertainty of appearance in a phrase universe.

The subject of Marker's ciné-roman is unable to forget "the sudden roar" [*overhead long shot*] dark underbelly of a plane in the air after takeoff. "the woman's gesture la geste de la femme" [Oh no!—Look out!—Keep away!—Come here quickly!], her fists thrown up against her face stifling [*out of it*] a laugh. Meeting the actor-Ghost she could be trying to stop *h a* escape. Her fingers spread open [*visage selvedge*] both shield and express. "Les clameurs des gens . . . ." He veers to the left "et que cet instant. . . ." Oh quickly! "Where [is] the soul?" [and beautiful] How is it contrived? "L'homme qui l'avait suivi depuis le camp souterrain—" [*run FLIGHT-LEFT reach out HAWK-WING-ARM*] What are your hands thrown up against? Did he give himself away? [*I do not ask you who you are not.*] Where did the protagonist go? [*there is no crowd, only the faces of that couple who may be his parents*] everyone is looking some- where else [*turned away from the runway not facing the camera.*] >Guardrail in half-light [*a plane on the ground arriving or depart- ing*] Sirens. {ellipse [Now] spliced on a land of promise <but now> There are no moorings in conversation. [Where is your soul? [-] "a crumbling body."

Fall fall my entire weight <bow>

VI

I showed views of Russia: Moscow, the Kremlin, the coronation—and some scenes of France. The Tsar professed great interest and asked many questions concerning the mechanism. I explained, and offered him a fragment of film. He held it up to the light, looking through it, and passed the strip from hand to hand. He thanked me and wished me success with the Lumière invention in Russia.
—Felix Mesguich, 1897[3]

1962. *Ivan's Childhood* opens, before the credits, with the solitary song of an unseen bird and a child's sunlit peacetime dream-image of a woman, his mother, smiling. The film, based on "Ivan," a popular wartime short story by Vladimir Bogomolov, had been poorly produced at the Mosfilm Studios when Andrei Tarkovsky, only recently graduated from the Institute of Cinematography, remade it. "I am simply in love with the subject. I was his age when the war began. His situation is that of my generation," he later wrote. He took the visual dream imagery for Ivan's first dream from one of his own early memories of summer in the Ukraine by the Dnieper river, before World War II. We see Ivan's face behind a spiderweb between the branches of a tree. Ivan sees a butterfly and follows it. The camera sweeps and pans over the forest, over the sandy bank of a river. His mother comes into view carrying a pail of water from the well. He runs to meet her. She sets the pail down. He dips his face in the water to get cool. "Mum, there's a cuckoo!" he tells her. She raises her arm over her forehead as if to wipe away sweat and listens with him. Her loving expression is the essence, the very play, of happiness. No voiceover settles linear sequentiality, though sounds do refer to what we see. In a standard pastoral fusion of music, bird songs, and running water, Ivan's high boyish

3 Quoted in Jay Leyda, *Kino: A History of the Russian and Soviet Film* (Macmillan, 1960, new ed. 1973), 22.

laughter, repeated and repeated, acts as a pivot. Speech represents logical human contact. In *Ivan's Childhood*, spontaneous acoustic signals of delight are hints of immanent reversal. Laughter uncannily suggests a coming breach.

Ivan's image of happiness has no black leader for shelter.

More than twenty million Russians died between 1941 and 1945. Some of the worst fighting of the war took place in the Ukraine between the Dniester and the Dnieper. Ivan was only dreaming. His mother's happy prewar expression cuts to terror. This look wakes him up. Now it is outside-inside freezing winter cramped shelter. *Now* is brute fact. Now he is dressed in a ragged padded jacket and cap. He is hiding in a shed or ruin then slogging through a swamp through blackened stumps and thickets. He has no mother. Death outstripped her life and will cut his memory out soon. In wartime she is foreign to representation. She only returns in dreams. When her son stops sleeping she will leave no trace. In Bogomolov's story, Lieutenant Galtsev is Ivan's witness. Nikolai Burlyaev, then a schoolboy in Moscow, acts the role of the skinny twelve-year-old orphaned reconnaissance scout. Many actors made screen tests for the part. Tarkovsky later wrote: "I had noticed Kolya, the future Ivan, when I was still a student. It is no exaggeration to say that my acquaintance with him decided my attitude to the filming."[4] The director doesn't explain what he means by this. The young actor who plays Galtsev reminds me of David, who was only twenty-three during the time he was a second lieutenant. In *La Jetée* the boy who may become the man marked by a memory from childhood may or may not be an actor. The three blonde children in *Sans Soleil* are three blonde children

4 Andrei Tarkovsky, *Sculpting in Time*, trans. Kitty Hunter-Blair (University of Texas Press, 1986), 33. Further citations are given with the abbreviation ST.

living in Iceland. According to the voiceover, spoken by a woman, the cameraman, who may or may not have been Marker, wasn't shooting a film at the time. He captured their images while on his travels because they represented for him the image of happiness. Footage of black volcanic ash covering their village, near the end of the film, was shot later by another documentarist. Still later *Sans Soleil's* semifictional narrator-cinematographer-correspondent tells his semifictional feminine voiceover: "History advances, plugging its memory as one plugs one's ears . . . A moment stopped would burn like a flame of film blocked before the furnace of the projector."

VII

In the middle of this warm prewar Sunday, where he could now stay.
—Chris Marker, *La Jetée*

Yesterday words could come between the distance. Frame light, for example. All living draw near. Knowing no data no something then something. No never and no opposite occident orient. Film with jumps and quick cuts. Dissolves and slide effects. Real chalk. Burnt-out ruins. Without weariness. Without our working conditions. When our forces hadn't been thrown.

What is valid documentary? In the long struggle who transmits the Diaspora?

Kolya, the future Ivan, David, my future husband, pick up the receiver. Real children on a peacetime morning before ruin. No sequence of dust fire smoldering ash. Just back to morning. The June of Everything.

Where in the flame does a film stop time?

VIII

Morning is the time of Midnight. Artificial Day

Some of my earliest memories are film memories confused with facts.

During the 1940s, the confusion or juxtaposition between living truth or acting life, always a part of the double and paradoxical nature of movie-going, involved a guilty reading-effect for American children whose fathers were away fighting as opposed to traveling in Europe Africa the South Pacific.

Murder with clock striking cat scurrying woman screaming.

Historical or geographical accident isolated us from the cold reality of mud and hunger. We were spectators chewing popcorn in a second darkness out of daylight looking at film-fact on one side of the screen not the other sides of oceans.

Superimposition of time: cinema-time immediate-time.

A film you love when you are young is never what you know you saw. Apparently cinema helps to reduce the distortion between a "dear" father and a "dead" father. It's the scene of horror the camera returns to, never the daughter.
"But we are lucky."
In fact space is imaginary.

During the 1940s, children in Cambridge, Massachusetts, went to the University Movie Theater on Saturday morning at 10 a.m. We saw newsreels, cartoons, previews of coming attractions, and a double feature.
We didn't talk. We divided the crime from the scene of it.

IX

Acts and Monuments.

In wartime zoo animals get scarce. Human destiny in the space of money. This world of fatherlands is covered in wounds. Subjects await their colonists. Trying to escape being crushed by a propeller I was searching for someone else. A wing flew open. The image through death.

All the war in the nonacted cinema.

BOMBER SUBMARINE BATTLESHIP NIGHT-ATTACK FIRE-BOMB INFANTRY TORPEDO DOODLE BUG KAMIKAZE: The camera may move along the sidewalk it's still a picture. GESTAPO HIMMLER HITLER GÖRING BAMBI TARZAN JANE: What Eurydice? Love is illusory.

"Can I piece the falling together?"

"David or Ivan."

"Oh it's you."

Banished from the Land of Children.

X

The Negative of Time

Dear Bae & Bill—

Your nice long letter came today, Bae. You asked about the country here. It is bleak and barren. It is real desert with none of the mountains we had around Oxnard. However, it is good country for flying and the weather is great. There are amazing sunrises. I think New Mexico is famous for them. The sky is full of bright colors. Orange, pink, and green. It is really amazing. We take off in the morning as soon as it is light and it is a very dramatic sight. Last week my instructor and three of us cadets took a cross-country to Dallas, Texas, for navigation practice. Dallas is about five hundred miles away. Cross-country trips like that are a lot like a cruise in a boat. Of course a cruise would be nicer. But when we get into bigger airplanes and they have a range of thousands of miles which they can travel in a relatively short time it will be better.

XI

This soil'd world
—Walt Whitman, "Reconciliation"

"Don't be worried by the sound of 'test pilot,'" David wrote home to his father and mother in 1943. "It is nothing glamorous or exciting like the movies make it sound. There are perfectly routine checks which must be made on all the airplanes at certain intervals. That is all there is to it." What he was really learning to do he learned to leave out. Less than a year later he was flying B-17s or "Flying Fortresses" on bombing missions over Germany in what military strategists, historians, and war buffs refer to as "the European Theater of War." Each letter a soldier wrote home from the "Theater" was inspected first by War Department censors. On the march only a language of remains gets past. All lost material in nonacted newsreels here is the real, the coverless.

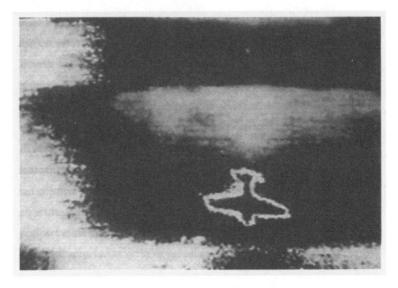

On September 7, 1938, Dziga Vertov listed among forbidden battle techniques of a documentarist: "Substituting the appearance of truth for truth itself" (KE 216).

Since David died I can look at photographs of him, though I still haven't been able to look at the video copy of a home movie his daughter sent us in 1991. It was filmed by his first wife's uncle during a summer in the 1950s. Bae was still alive. She died October 9, 1965, so I never met her. Here she sits on a garden chair in Ogunquit in summer. She is reading, knitting, or watching her granddaughter, Lisa. Judging from family photograph albums, her husband was usually surrounded by admiring painting students and fellow artists. In this homemade film Bae is a widow in her sixties. I remember that in our last summer together David couldn't look at the recovered black-and-white-film documentation of her moving image without crying. Sometimes he and Lisa's mother are playing in the sand with their daughter. Sometimes he stands at the door of his studio then goes inside. He designed the building himself. Now it has been torn down. I can only perceive its imprint or trace. Lisa remembers listening to the noise of waves breaking over pebbles in the cove at night, how tides pulled them under, how they swirled and regrouped in the drift and came back.

I imagine the noise as fixity gathering like a heartbeat, steady and sure.

I have pushed the video-cassette box onto the bookshelf near your desk, out of sight. Because the camera operates at sixteen frames per second for old home movies, and speed is silent. Because your moving image would rupture the suture of sound projection. Because there is no acoustic parallel, nor is concord possible. *"The bad old days"*; mocking scramble for cover torn labor.

October 5, 1993, October of meeting nowhere.

On January 21, 1924, Vladimir Ilich Lenin suffered a massive stroke. He died that evening at 6:50. We close the mouth and the eyes of the dead and arrange their bodies so they look as if they are sleeping peacefully or resting before we burn, bury, or seal them up.

Lenin's body lay in his sickroom at Gorki on a sheet-draped table surrounded by flowers and fir branches. During the night friends, colleagues, and relatives stood guard over his remains. The following day his body was placed in a coffin lined with red cloth, a small red pillow under his head. Pallbearers and mourners carried the coffin to the train and boarded it. When the train reached Moscow, where the dead leader was to lie in state, the route to the Trade Union House with its Hall of Columns was lined with troops. The temperature was forty degrees below zero, but crowds were gathered on streets, rooftops, balconies, everywhere. The hall was draped with black and red ribbons, black banners hung from the ceilings. The coffin was carried from the train by Kalinin, Bukharin, Tomsky, Kamenev, Stalin, Rudzutak, Zinoviev, and Rykov. Over half a million people filed by his bier between January 23 and 26. Outside the temperatures were freezing, yet they stood for hours night and day waiting for a chance to look. In *Lenin Lives! The Lenin Cult in Soviet Russia*, Nina Tumarkin describes Lenin's bizarre progress from mortal revolutionary hero to embalmed cult-icon under glass. It wasn't easy; there were technical and scientific embalming problems, competitions for best sarcophagus designs, committees. In November 1930 the granite porphyry and labradorite mausoleum holding the transparent coffin opened to the public.

"Modern tombs are a skeptical affair . . . the ancient sculptors have left us nothing to say in regard to the great, final contrast." When Henry James wrote this he was referring to the art of stone, not the art of moving pictures.

Throughout 1933, eagerly or devotedly following Lenin's instruction that "the production of new films inspired by Communist ideas and reflecting Soviet reality should begin with the newsreel," Vertov labored to produce *Three Songs about Lenin*, commissioned for the tenth anniversary of their leader's death. In preparation he and Elizaveta Svilova searched through "archival, cinematheque and unprocessed footage" in various cities including Tiflis, Kiev, and Baku, for moving images of the living Lenin that might have been overlooked by newsreel editors. "In each instance the brunt of the work involved in exploring gigantic amounts of archive footage fell on Svilova's shoulders. For the tenth anniversary of Lenin's death she particularly distinguished herself, when, through a painstaking examination of hundreds of thousands of feet of film in various archives and storehouses, she not only located shots essential for [the project] but reported finding, in addition, ten original negatives that render the living Ilyich on film" (KE 153). With the help of a new sound engineer, P. Shtro, they were able, during one brief climactic section, to transfer Lenin's voice to film. Utilitarian pragmatism, iconoclasm, Constructivism, pomposity, sentimentalism, modernity, archaism, and strident nationalism can all be located in this cinematographic memorial with its vivid musical score by I. Shaporin.

"FIRST SONG (hand lettered) 'Under a Black Veil My Face ...'"[5]

Vertov and Svilova collated their newly collected archival documentary material with other footage already gathered between 1919 and 1924 by the Council of Three, or Kinoki (the third member of the triumvirate was the cameraman, Vertov's brother, Mikhail Kaufman). This was juxtaposed with ethnographic segments photographed by D. Sourenski, M. Magidson, and B. Monastyrsky, of women, almost completely shrouded under layers of clothing, from the eastern areas of the Soviet Union. Sometimes, these walking mummies joyfully fling off the veils covering their faces, for the camera. Other women are shown learning to shoot rifles, entering workers' clubs, learning to read, learning to operate heavy machinery.

5 Annette Michelson, "The Kinetic Icon in the Work of Mourning: Prolegomena to the Analysis of a Textual System," *October* 52 (Spring 1990), 43. Further citations are given with the abbreviation O.

Three Songs about Lenin was produced in 1933 during the unsettling period of transition between silent film and film with synchronous sound. For the first two Songs it's as if two realities are being unified and falsified by the controlling musical score and instructional titles superimposed. By the third Song the materialist conception of history is no longer a hypothesis but a scientifically demonstrated proposition with an understanding of the potentials of the microphone. On the level of subject matter the internalized danger situation of a lost love-object is being projected, printed, and distributed throughout.

Sound effects seesaw through artifices of montage.

Turkish, Turkmen, and Uzbek folk songs about Lenin are hailing a worldview that the old materialism could not satisfy. Late nineteenth-century Romanticism, Siegfried's funeral music from Wagner's *Götterdammerung*, is hailing a delayed reaction to Hegel's faith in human reason. The practical telecommunication of the mid-twentieth century is hailing. "Hey, you there!"

December 1932, an efficient machine interrupted by the assassination of Kirov. Other people against the wall. All this behind-the-scenes in the World Market. "Hey, you there!"

Lenin's insistent communicativeness.

"How many times here in the Red Square—" / "—did we hear him speak?" (O 43)

In the middle of the second Song there is a sequence where the Founder of the Soviet Union, in the very act of haranguing the masses with his raised arm, interrupts the officious narrative commentary. As if he really could be projecting his aggressive instincts on the restrictions of cinematographic plausibility, Lenin, mouthpiece source and limit of realism, talks.

Stress the importance of triumph. Poignancy of its imagos.

Learning to talk is a complicated process. The child's growing skill between two realist poles, hostile impulses as well as "bad" internal objects; a little demon of melodrama. Helping figures quickly blossom in the creative surge of aesthetic necessity. Yes the triumph of split-off illusion no the ambush and defeat.

Some of the mourners are acting looking back.

"THIRD SONG (hand lettered) 'In Moscow. . .' / 'Ah, in the great city of stone. . .' / 'On the square stands a "tent". . .' / 'The "tent" where Lenin lies. . .'" We see workers inspired by "The Country's First Great Electrificator Lenin," laboring joyfully in huge hydroelectric plants, in factories, on collective farms. "'Machinery is now the weapon. . .' / 'OUR OIL!' / 'OUR COAL!' / 'OUR METAL!' / 'Our mighty Baltic-White Sea Canal. . .' / 'Lenin, we go FORWARD!'" (O 50-51). While the message may be that Leninist-Communism is liberating, particularly so for women, Annette Michelson demonstrates in "The Kinetic Icon in the Work of Mourning: Prolegomena to the Analysis of a Textual System," ways in which this film she calls "a veritable iconostasis" draws its subliminal visionary force by working in and around the ancient Russian tradition, through music, iconography, and literature, of anonymous female oral lamentation at funerals and burial ceremonies.

If, as Melanie Klein says, following Freud, mourning is the pain experienced in the slow process of testing reality, *Three Songs about Lenin* is a cinematographic embodiment of the fluid and passing states, the interaction and interjection, between sorrow and distress. This innovative postrevolutionary cinematic memorial to the father of the socialist motherland, by use of the camera's eye, may bring into arbitrary relief the patient mitigation of hatred by love. But why do women in moving pictures so often serve as representations of the extension of love united before strife, at the same time they are being "caught unawares" by the camera's point of view?

Writing this essay I have no clear idea what value there can be in a fragment of concrete reality in itself multiple and always at the mercy of a national and personal identity. The real time of emotion isn't musical time or background noise of civilization or continuity of exposed film. You can always tell memory, not the coverings it closes first.

Three Songs about Lenin runs forward by half removes into those early blacklist days, wonderfully without defense.

Defense as it appears in fortresses and humans.

La Jetée is made up almost entirely of stills. It opens with a lowering sun, departing planes, and World War III about to begin. Marker's use of photograms and freeze frames in this film that calls itself a fiction is a compelling documentation of the interaction and multiple connections perceived separately and at once between lyric poetry and murderous history. That's the secret meaning. I knew it by telepathy in 1948 when I was eleven and first saw the movie of *Hamlet*. André Bazin says in "Theater and Cinema": "When a character moves off screen, we accept the fact he is out of sight, but he continues to exist in his own capacity at some other place in the decor which is hidden from us. There are no wings to the screen."[6]

Chris Marker's filmography lists a twenty-six-minute video, "Tarkovski '86," as part of a longer work called *Zapping*

6 André Bazin, *What Is Cinema?*, ed. and trans. Hugh Gray (University of California Press, 1967), 105.

Zone. I haven't been able to see it, but I noticed his name on the list of credits at the end of the ponderously titled *The Genius, The Man, The Legend: Andrei Tarkovsky*, produced by the Swedish Film Institute in 1988.

Tarkovsky directed a stage production of *Hamlet* in 1976. "To begin with, it's a family, a closely-knit family, they mustn't have the slightest inkling of all that lies ahead of them. They are very protective of each other, very dear to each other, they are all together. And that makes them happy!" he wrote in reference to Ophelia, Laertes, and Polonius in act 1, scene 3.[7]

The Russian director Andrei Tarkovsy often mixed documentary footage with fiction. He scattered professional actors, stagehands, friends, and family members throughout his films just as he arbitrarily blended time periods with international and domestic situations. The project he variously titled, *A White, White Day, Atonement, Redemption, Why Are You Standing So Far Away*, even *Martyrology*, was to include fragments of straight interviews between his mother, Maria Ivanova, who had once been an actress, and himself, until he abandoned this early cinema-vérite approach and replaced the interview format with acted scenes. *Mirror* is partially based on his memories and her memories of life before, during, and after the war. The actress Margarita Terekhova plays both his wife and his mother, while Maria Ivanova is herself and acts her mother. Ignat Daniltsev plays Tarkovsky's son Ignat (really Andriuska) and Alexi (Andrei himself) as a boy. Oleg Yankovsky is the director's film father, while his real father's poems are read off-screen by Arseny himself. Real or acting, the characters have the same reflection in whichever mirror serves as camera for the filmmaker for his

7 Andrei Tarkovsky, *Time within Time: The Diaries, 1970–1986*, trans. Kitty Hunter-Blair (Verso, 1993), 381.

cinematographer. They can pass back and forth from one to the other but that's what movie acting is because there are no wings to the screen any soul can be the body.

Distant woods beautiful auspicious morning at evening a sudden west wind soughing through white flowering meadow. Facts are perceptions of surfaces.

In *Sculpting in Time*, Tarkovsky writes about his problems beginning *Mirror*. First it was to be a novella about the wartime evacuation, with the plot centering on a military instructor at his school. During the second version of the script the idea of the interview with his mother took precedence, "but the incident. . . continued to torment me, and lived on in my memory until it had become a minor episode of the film"(ST 128-29). He abandoned the second version because he continued to feel he was missing an essential vision or fact or memory that would raise the project above the level of lyrical autobiography. The constantly changing quality of this work in progress confirmed his feeling that scenario is fragile and constantly changes with the material as well as with qualities individual actors bring to it. This improvisational way of working continued throughout the filming and editing stages. At some point he decided to include newsreel shots, though he seems to have been worried about the combination of acted and documentary sequences. He gathered found footage intending to use it, but the collection represented only isolated fragments lacking the single time-sense he wanted. So, just as Vertov and Svilova had done while preparing *Three Songs about Lenin*, he continued searching, until the day he came across a sequence showing Soviet soldiers crossing Lake Sivash. "Suddenly—quite unheard of for a newsreel—here was a record of one of the most dramatic moments in the history of the Soviet advance of 1943. It was a unique piece; I could hardly believe that such an enormous footage of film should have been spent recording one single event continuously observed. It had clearly been filmed by a gifted camera-man. When, on the screen before me, there appeared, as if coming out of nothing, these people shattered by the fearful, inhuman effort of that tragic moment of history, I knew that this episode had to become the centre, the very essence, heart, nerve of this picture that had started off merely as my intimate lyrical memories" (ST 130). The army cameraman who filmed this extraordinary document was killed the same day he shot the footage. Tarkovsky doesn't give us his name. I haven't been able to find it in any writing about the film. Most of the young soldiers were killed also. The Soviet chief of State Cinema advised him to remove the sequence from the wider selection of documentary intervals or detours because the scene showed too much suffering.

When, almost halfway through the film, the director begins to introduce the various black-and-white newsreel documentary inserts, they telescope together, binding his memory-time of youth to the actual geopolitical chain of violence, seemingly everywhere during the second half of the twentieth century. The archival inserts are sometimes shown at a slower speed, sometimes with "wild recording" faked later.

Sent-back poems from the invisible side of events.

The newsreel filmed by the anonymous cameraman at Lake Sivash acts as an open parenthesis for the tragicomic autobiographical episode in which evacuated boys, at target practice in an icy outdoor rifle-range, play a cruel joke on their shell-shocked military instructor. He has no name either.

In fact authentic documentary material blighted the hearts of children all over the world who came to consciousness enveloped by threatened futurity, during the non-nuclear and then nuclear 1940s. We were alert to the subliminal disjunction between actual and fictional cinematographic realism shown in theaters (never called cinemas) because no one had television at home. When I said that in Cambridge, on Saturdays at 10 a.m., the weekly ritual for children at the University Movie Theater consisted of a newsreel, a cartoon, previews, the main feature, and a serial, I left out the intermission. The curtain came down, as if this were a play, and much to our disgust, perhaps because it demonstrated in fact there were wings to the screen, a real man—comedian or magician, his name didn't matter, we never knew it—walked onstage with a blackboard and other props. We scorned him for interrupting our absorption in ritual. We scorned him for being human. "Let's get on with the show! Let's get on with the show!" I chanted with the crowd firing tickets, spitballs, and popcorn in his direction, no matter that some of us had been sobbing over the death of noble animals in *My Friend Flicka* or *Bob, Son of Battle* not ten minutes earlier. During wartime, quantities of aggressive impulses nullified our terror of the danger of disruption and released our obsessional defense mechanisms. We needed to show triumph, so we persecuted this mortal parenthesis with hoots and jeers. Saturday after Saturday he recited the number lists and little miracles that made up his repertoire of tricks or jokes, until the lights dimmed, he carried his props offstage to the margins from whence he came, and the curtain rose revealing the screen. The soul had returned to the body, the main feature could resume.

According to the narrator of *Sans Soleil*, the baffling part of the Japanese Shinto ritual of Dondo-yaki is that circle of little boys we see shouting and beating the litter of scraps of burnt ornaments or votive offerings with long sticks after the flames have died down. They tell him it's to chase away the moles. He sees it as a small intimate service.

In English *mole* can mean, aside from a burrowing mammal, a mound or massive work formed of masonry and large stones or earth laid in the sea as a pier or breakwater. Thoreau calls a pier a "noble mole" because the sea is silent but as waves wash against and around it they sound and sound is language.

Specimen Days, published in 1882, consists of extracts from notebooks Walt Whitman kept between 1862 and 1865 when he was visiting sick and wounded soldiers on the field and in hospitals around Washington, D.C. There are other sequences in Specimen Days he calls memoranda, later added in Camden, New Jersey, where the poet moved after suffering his first paralytic stroke. One, "pencill'd . . . one warm October noon," titled "Cedar-Plums Like—Names," is about the problem he had naming the book. In a footnote marked by an asterisk he provides a list of suggested and rejected titles. There are thirty-five. "Then reader dear, in conclusion, as to the point of the name for the present collection, let us be satisfied to have a name—something to identify and bind it together, to concrete all its vegetable, mineral, personal memoranda, abrupt raids of criticism, crude gossip of philosophy, varied sands clumps—without bothering ourselves because certain pages do not present themselves to you or me as coming under their own name with entire fitness or amiability." As if to stifle his own egotism, he adds, in parenthesis: "(It is a profound, vexatious, never-explicable matter—this of names. I have been exercised deeply about it my whole life.)"[8]

Children know by precognition how precariously names cling to civilization. In order to qualify for language they must stifle unrelenting internalization. "We have a message for you—our spirits being out of body." Images have countries whose streets they cannot fathom. Immense stretches of ocean up to this frame the screen.

"I just dreamed of you mama. By the way when did father leave us?"

"1935, why?"

Mirror: *The Newsreel Sequences*

history does run backwards through endless generations of murderers. The Spanish Civil War zooms in on us because in cinema people do talk from the grave

eating away at character because public evaluation is troublesome and wants autobiographical fiction. No the camera

8 Walt Whitman, *Complete Poetry and Collected Prose*, ed. Justin Kaplan (Library of America, 1982), 886.

pulls away from corresponding impressions lyric pulls away. No the benign circle shed also. Time itself running through though shot not smoothly but by jolt by static energy. Checking the cost. No the collision of one objective nonacted group shot with another.

No by the very facts.

A woman walks quickly down a city sidewalk carrying a long pane of broken glass. It's a window not a mirror. Bombs are being dropped from planes. Do they fly across the screen from left to right because we read in that direction? Cut to bombs exploding though we only hear singing. Two women, one carrying a bouquet of flowers, run for cover. Other citizens are seeking shelter. Theater for whom? Some half glance at the camera as they hurry in

meanwhile the angry retrospective nostalgia of flamenco music on the soundtrack reiterates the place of Spain while bridging the transition between acted and nonacted scenes. As if by impasse of idealization cinema can reestablish security and life itself and song will soothe we will be soothed to silently watch these incessant relentless negative retrievements this debris rayed over.

Frantic grown-ups are evacuating groups of children probably from Madrid. It's a question of security but who will love them don't that's the substitute part. All the pain of the world is concentrated in this place crammed with people dear to each other. He tries to comfort his mother before going. His father kisses and kisses him. What do you see camera?

Shouts and not memorized.

Some children haul heavy suitcases, some wear identification badges, some kiss their relations good-bye, some set off eagerly some are sobbing. A young boy uses a large white pocket handkerchief to wipe away his tears. Cries of love and alarm on the soundtrack fade into an air-raid siren, factory whistle, or is it the whistle of a train approaching.

We are as real and near as cinema.

A little girl, half-turned away holding her doll, smiles shyly. When the ambiguous siren or engine wails its warning she turns directly towards the camera. Medium close-up her expression changing to a mixture of astonishment or terror. This child is not acting. Perhaps she knows what the young actor in *Ivan's Childhood* pretends he knows.

Her look pierces the mask of western culture.

(Almost forty years later, in June, 1972, a terrified Phan Thi Kin Phuc, napalmed in error by a South Vietnamese bomber, will come running naked down a road, having torn off her burning clothing.

She is running towards the camera's single eye.)

A man without wings swings slantingly into view through free space mute sky

1 2 3 4 5 6 seconds of silent soundtrack before liturgical music through fade-in to a certain point then tapering emitting wave notes risen from years of other powers. Balancing and hovering he is swinging in a basket as if re-entrance is easy. Swings in again coming home so it's a picture projected through time subtler than poems or a letter because he is working on

it. Found footage shown at slower speed here is power. A tremendous stratosphere spinnaker so weightless after the weighty Spanish evacuation sequence hovers preparing for lift-off well he needs no map to return if fiction angel astronaut returning to home base as if he merely floated out of sight for fun as if reentrance is possible and surely there are to be anchorage mooring helpers waiting. Star boat USSR

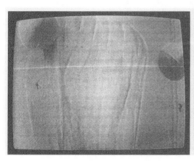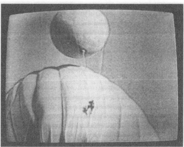

resembles a light sail of great speed used on yachts when running before the wind, spinnaker because a yacht called *Sphinx* carried such a sail in 1866. Utilitarian loveliness, a huge bubble of nylon pulling tons of boat through water, but sometimes relentless swinging and thrashing shakes the rig out of her tugging

now the spinnaker is drawing now the long chase ahead. Coming next will be other newsreel footage of young soldiers slogging through mud and shallow water not doing well exhausted though one or two smile wanly at the camera

I wish you could see this film. Sometimes I recognize you inside it so scared and young always among those Soviet

soldiers who are crossing Lake Sivash why should there be
twice as many sick as wounded

you float back to me everything inexpressible

aerodynamic repair experiment for the freshly washed
white star boat USSR getting ashore to let you sleep well. Light
sail of great spread used on yachts when running before the
wind.
Once you could cover my hand completely with your
palm.

A huge bubble of nylon pulling tons of boat through
skywater swinging and thrashing relentless threatening to
shake the rig out now tugging water now touched by science
now drawing silence inside the long chase ahead.
Scenes like this men use

clinging vine method to hang on filling out running
before the wind but here there is no yacht and open ocean is
air. The effect is the same flying-jib out astride the small boom
so spinnaker to get north. Smaller balloons circle and touch the
mother one as satellites do then sacred chorus singing sanctus
sanctus. All is well. Melody for a while. Melodies antedate lan-
guages they do not grow old. A peaceful weightless wingless
furlough one or two other balloons revolve around these
smaller powers after peace.

One aerialist sailor attached by a string to a satellite
balloon floats in and down across the screen from right to left

where are his supports as child attached to a mother? As if he were returning home again a crowd to watch and applaud so from heaven he smiles. Where are you systems of planets around us? Drifting out of sight away out of the frame of the screen behind the wings. Annihilation is the deep chaos answer sheets and white film turmoil. It's a separation wish to be carried out also as if to silence of ether. Irrationality of speech to surrender the beauty of this voyage without baggage to shed earth. Because our fathers have not kept their word. Artificers and builders convey to one another someone was thought to be worthy. Colorlessness prefigures a connection when the unconscious mind mirrors love-partners who are in absolute contrast but by early influence that the child had had time her impressions of her father may have been shaken if there ever was a way to translate the *feeling* of image-juxtaposition in these words moving from left to right across this sheet of paper.

Nicely coordinated teamwork between camera crew director actors *Mirror* the private life.

The sea is a theater.

Steerage toward redemptive bourgeois historical resolution what music to windward probably unaware of rocks the motion of waves the swelling fold how quickly the sail becomes a contorted mass of fabric.

Sequences touched off by and surrounding the originary memory of the military instructor without a name. His overanxiousness to keep all his pupils safe. He is a teacher and then about the worry that so perfectly matches these restless boundaries of realism.

Come tell us *young* man.

We can't hear him crying his excessive sorrow because of the world. He has resigned himself in phobia projections and defenses for love. Nothing can remove that split in the film it's too close the masters have been mixed. Double the safe place death. You can see the dramatic force of this central counterpoint ellipse. You know the joke of the boy who tosses the dummy hand-grenade onto the boards. You know the instructor will become the nerve to throw himself down in order to save his young pupils (he is a teacher he thinks he would die for them that sense of omnipotence).

(You hear his heartbeat louder and louder sometimes to the point of martyrdom

Of course the hand-grenade never explodes though his beating heart does change to the beating of drums to a drum-roll marshaling. Poor man this excess of activity no nurse by his side no friend to assist him in his struggles. Some are so young and already representative of current events we are bound to confront

I'll summon a century
at will,

juxtaposed with the newsreel footage, shot by the anonymous cameraman. Soldiers of the Soviet Army slogging through the shallow water and mud flats of Lake Sivash, the "Putrid Sea," in the Russian advance of 1943. During the final shots of this sequence the auteur-director's father, the poet Arseny Tarkovsky's voiceover recitation of his Whitmanesque poem "Life Life" lends a piercing sadness to these sepia image-traces of patience, fortitude, desperate fatigue, legs stiff from damp and chill, young faces looking blankly at the eye of the camera, the steady, silent, progress forward across seemingly endless shallows. Some of the men are hauling a barge carrying wheels and guns so heavy what could ever be more unlike the floating stratosphere sequence but its the same war. *No need / To be afraid of death at seventeen / Nor yet at seventy.* Noise of water sloshing synchronized later no extraneous breathing or irrelevant sound-wave energy. *Reality and light / Exist, but neither death nor darkness.* Floating currency. All of us are on the sea-shore now. Drum roll percussion echo reverberation. *And I am one of those who haul the nets / When a shoal of immortality comes in.* Who are the oldest principal officers? *Live in the house—and the house will stand. / I will call up any century, / Go into it and build myself a house.* (ST 143) Almost everyone keeps walking, continually proceeding.

The next newsreel footage inserts, juxtaposed with another memory sequence, the young Leningrad blockade orphan and his evacuee companions playing in snow, date from 1945 and after. Antitank guns at night. A banner flapping and snapping. Documentarist shooting dead Nazi. A man with a crutch cowering in a makeshift bomb shelter he could nearly be weeping.

Ardmore Airforce Base
Ardmore, OKLA
Monday, April 12, 1945

Dear Bae & Bill

A little while ago I heard the terrible news about the President's death. What a blow to the world!

This has been an exciting night. There has been a thunderstorm and there were cyclones all around us. But things are quiet now and everything will be OK.

Americans exploded the first atomic bomb at Alamogordo, New Mexico, July 16, 1945 at sunrise. Heat from the blast fused the surrounding desert sand to glass.

Was the next quick newsreel sequence in *Mirror* shot shortly before 8:15 a.m., August 6, 1945? Are those young fliers in the cockpit piloting the *Enola Gay*? Are they on their mission to explode the secret uranium weapon known as Little Boy?

(A little boy who survived Hiroshima remembered the moment the bomb fell, a red dragonfly, the sound of a B-29, his brother reaching out to catch a dragonfly and a flash: "It's strange, those fragmentary scenes remain fixed in my mind like photographs.")

We could be seeing footage from a later test at Bikini Island in the Pacific; in that one some G.I.s were lethally exposed. Maybe the fireball mushroom cloud is from the plutonium one the United States army exploded over Nagasaki on August 9, 1945.

Cut. Gunfire. Flak. Roar. Smoke. Chinese political rally hands waving totalitarian saluting. Sheets of glass framing portraits of Mao. Little icon-busts of Mao. Books leaflets. Mao's little red book. His face on the cover. The Sino-Soviet split. Soviet soldiers forming a human chain to keep oriental peoples back. Some of them shove forward waving photos of Mao. A vast political outdoor ceremony somewhere probably China.

In *La Jetée* and *Mirror*, also in *Sans Soleil*, one finds images associated with, or rising from, Hiroshima. I don't think you can grasp the hauntedness in all of them without understanding this central surrender of soul, in its nuclear plight forgetting and refusing to forget.

The immense indifference of history. The crushing hold of memory's abiding present. Compared to facts words are only nets. We go on hauling in what traces of affirmation we can catch. Action is the movement of memory searching for a lost attachment a make-believe settlement. A screen is a sort of mole or sea wall. It keeps spirit back.

Thus in silence in dreams' projections,
—Walt Whitman, "The Wound-Dresser"

XII
Because I know that time is always time
And place is always and only place
—T. S. Eliot, *Ash-Wednesday*

This is the epigraph to the English-language version of *Sans Soleil*, released for distribution in the United States in 1982. Documentary and experimental films have a hard time being distributed in North America. Sadly, these films seem to reach only a cosmopolitan coterie of filmmakers, artists, photographers, and film scholars. It's the same situation with experimental poetry. Books and magazines of or about non-mainstream poetry are consigned chiefly to small-press distribution networks or cooperatives, and few bookstores order them.

I thought first about writing something on documentaries about poets because I remembered the recent PBS *Voices and Visions* series, now subtitled for distribution: "A Television Course on Modern American Poetry." The series consists of thirteen one-hour video programs "presenting the life and work of major American poets." I was curious why most of them seemed so flat, though the word "major" was an alert. After watching them all again, this time taking notes, I couldn't think of anything to say. Mike Cartmell, a Canadian filmmaker, suggested I look at *Sans Soleil*. He described it as an autobiographical work about a French filmmaker with an assumed name. *Sans Soleil* wasn't about poetry; it was poetry, he said. I had just finished writing *The Birth-mark: Unsettling the Wilderness in American Literary History*. Marker collided with birth-mark, the assumed name struck home.

XIII

"So, montage is conflict." Several years ago I plucked this quotation from Eisenstein's "The Cinematographic Principle and the Ideogram" to use as an epigraph to an essay about

Charles Olson's *Call Me Ishmael: A Study of Melville*. Franklin D. Roosevelt's sudden death shocked Olson into completing the book he had been unable to pull together for years. Now he started over, cutting, juxtaposing and compressing his material in a radically new way. It was finished "before the 1st A-bomb, 1st week that August." August 6, 1945, marked a point in time after which nothing could be the same. A few months later Olson resigned his government positions (member of the Office of War Information in Washington and Director of the Foreign Nationalities Division of the Democratic National Committee). Olson's critical study of *Moby-Dick* marked his own delayed beginning as a poet.

Short cuts, mixed credits, news items, archival material, nonfictitious science, science fiction, pulp fiction, travel narratives, epigraphs, ballads, and passages from the Bible represent the delayed beginning of Herman Melville's *Moby-Dick*. First the effusive dedication to Hawthorne, next the "Etymology" and "Extracts" sections. Aside from the dedication, and possibly even there, all of these scattered particles of fact and or fable meet in the word-event *whale*.

Sans Soleil has a delayed beginning. Marker's film bares the device of its structure first. Credits, quotations, shots filmed by himself and others are spliced and surrounded with black leader. Even the title comes in three languages and colors. For a filmmaker a camera is a screen within a screen; so is a word to a poet. Shots of a Japanese temple consecrated to cats begin and end the main body of Marker's *Sunless* cycle. A couple has come to display an inscribed wooden slat in the cat cemetery in order to protect their missing cat Tora. We see rows of enigmatic porcelain cats, each with one paw raised, as if to deliver some incommunicable communication. Rituals for recovering lost or dead animals occur throughout the movie.

Herman Melville, Emily Dickinson, and Walt Whitman were all using montage before it was a word for a working method. Their writing practice (varied though it was) involved comparing and linking fragments or shots, selecting fragments for scenes, reducing multitudes (chapters or stanzas) and shots (lines and single words) to correlate with one another, constantly interweaving traces of the past to overcome restrictions of temporal framing. The influence Whitman had on Vertov through Mayakovsky is well known. Is the Melville who wrote *Typee, Omoo, Redburn*, "The Encantadas," and "Benito Cereno," a travel writer, a beachcomber, a reporter, or a poet? *Moby-Dick* is a poetic documentary fiction on a grand scale. Often I think of Dickinson's handwritten manuscripts as "Drawings in motion. Blueprints in motion. Plans for the future. The theater of relativity of the screen" (KE 9). With an important difference: if kino-eye signifies, among other things, the conquest of space—"I am kino-eye, I am a mechanical eye. I, a machine, show you the world only as I can see it" (KE 17)—Dickinson's pen-eye aims at the conquest of mechanical reproduction. It seems after reaching the age of consent she refused to be photographed.

Seventeenth- and eighteenth-century American Puritan theologians and historians like Roger Williams, Anne Bradstreet, and Cotton Mather were obsessed with anagrams. Seventeenth-century American Puritans were iconoclasts and animists at once. Ralph Waldo Emerson, Herman Melville, Emily Dickinson, T. S. Eliot, H.D., Marianne Moore, William Carlos Williams, Wallace Stevens, Charles Olson, and John Cage are among many North American writers who inherit this feeling for letters as colliding image-objects and divine messages. "Association, so far as the word stands for an effect, is between THINGS THOUGHT OF—it is THINGS, not ideas, which are associated in the mind. We ought to talk of the association of objects, not the association of ideas"—William James. "If he [the author] make of his volume a mole whereon the waves of Silence may break it is well"—Henry David Thoreau. Needing to translate words into THINGS THOUGHT OF could be the mark of a North American poet

if marks of scattered hues in October sunsets geographically here can ever be translated into English.

Walter Benjamin was also attracted to the idea that single letters in a word or name could be rearranged to cabalistically reveal a hidden purpose. "My thinking relates to theology the way a blotter does to ink. It is soaked through with it. If one were to go by the blotter, though, nothing of what has been written would remain."[9] It's sad to read that one of the reasons given for Benjamin's suicide in 1940 was his reluctance to emigrate to the United States.

Here he didn't expect to go anywhere.

A mark is the face of a fact. A letter is naked matter breaking from form from meaning. An anagram defies linear logic. Any letter of the alphabet may contain its particular indwelling spirit. A mark is a dynamic cut. Dynamic cutting is a highly stylized form of editing. Sequences get magpied together from optical surprises, invisible but omnipresent verbal flashes, flashes of facts. A documentary work is an attempt to

9 Walter Benjamin. "N [Re the Theory of Knowledge. Theory of Progress]," trans. Leigh Hafrey and Richard Sieburth, in *Benjamin, Philosophy, Aesthetics, History*, ed. Gary Smith (University of Chicago Press, 1989), 61.

recapture someone something somewhere looking back. Looking back, Orpheus was the first known documentarist: Orpheus, or Lot's wife.

> Wavering between the profit and the loss
> In this brief transit where the dreams cross
> —T. S. Eliot, *Ash-Wednesday*

An epigraph is an afterthought. Usually it follows the title of a work. An epigraph is second sight. Severed from its original position, replaced at a foreign margin, the magpied quotation now suggests a theme or acts as talisman. Magpies are pied: mostly black with white patches and white tail stripes. Harbingers of ill omen, they tend to be associated with thresholds and secret ministry. In Ireland, if we saw any, my mother taught us to count quickly: "One is for sorrow, two is for joy, three for a marriage, and four for a boy." The word magpie also refers to the black and white ceremonial dress of an Anglican bishop. In captivity magpies imitate human speech. An early English dictionary describes these members of the jay family as "the cleverest, the most grotesque, the most musical of crows." In 1852, *Webster's American Dictionary of the English Language* bluntly defines magpie: "a chattering bird of the crow tribe."

> Among twenty snowy mountains,
> The only moving thing
> Was the eye of the blackbird.
> —Wallace Stevens, "Thirteen Ways
> of Looking at a Blackbird"

People say the magpie has a spot of blood of the devil on its tongue.

People who like anagrams are usually attracted to epigraphs.

XIV

Léloignement des pays répare en quelque sorte la trop grande proximité des temps.
—Racine, *Seconde Préface à Bazajet*

Marker's epigraph to the original French version of *Sans Soleil* is lifted from Racine's second preface to *Bazajet*, one of the seventeenth-century dramatist's least-known works in English. *Bazajet* is a Turkish tragedy set in a seraglio. The magpied lines are the second part of a point Racine was making. "On peut dire que le respect que l'on a pour les héros augmente à mesure qu'ils s'éloignent de nous: *major e longinquo reverentia.*" [We may say the respect that we harbor for heroes increases in proportion to their distance from us.] What Marker didn't let in or cut out contains in itself a quotation without marks lifted by Racine from the *Annals* of the Roman historian Tacitus.

For Roland Barthes the essence of the Racinian eros is sight. In both *La Jetée* and *Sans Soleil* sight is privileged. The image takes the place of the thing. Erotic scenes could be hallucinations. "I see her, she saw me, she knows that I see her, she drops me her glance, just an angle, when it is still possible to act as though it was not addressed to me, and at the end the real glance straightforward that lasted a 24th of a second, the length of a film frame." In *La Jetée* and *Sans Soleil* as in a play by Racine, glances are the equivalents of interviews. A look can be an embrace or a wound. Even the gaze of statues.

XV

Laertes: *A document in madness: thoughts and remembrance fitted.*

The Capgras syndrome is rare. A patient believes that a person, usually closely related to her, has been replaced by an exact double. When it was first described in 1923 by Capgras and Reboul-Lachaux, they titled it *l'illusion des sosies.* In French, the term *sosie* comes from Plautus's *Amphitryon.* There the god Mercury assumes the appearance of Sosie, Amphitryon's servant, thus becoming his double.

Sans Soleil is supposed to be the autobiographical account of a traveling filmmaker named Sandor Krasna. The narrating voiceover is an anonymous woman, perhaps a film editor, a liaison officer, or a sister, remembering letters and camera footage mailed to her from faraway places by a documentarist who is or was a roving reporter. He could be an editor, collaborator, lover, teacher, student, brother, "Sandor Krasna," whatever. There is the suggestion that "he," as she always calls him (the credit list at the end supplies the name Krasna), has gone away somewhere, possibly forever. She (the credits say "Florence Delay") says what she says he wrote shows what she says he shot. We aren't sure who is real or imaginary; on the other hand, we understand him to be the cinematographer Chris Marker. Marker's filmography—*Lettre de Sibérie* (1957), *Cuba Si* (1961), *Le Joli Mai* (1962), *La Bataille des Dix Millions* (1970)—beckons his audience in the direction of cinema-verité. Chris Marker: Marxist cinematographer, always on the wing, not to be glimpsed except in flight, doesn't like to be photographed.

Marker's practice of cutting, isolating, grafting, and synthesizing music, languages, machine noises, musical synthesizers, and quotations (Marlon Brando's voice from *Apocalypse Now*) depends on invisible verbal flashes, optical surprises, and split images. Ophelia's mad song evokes Jean Simmons in Olivier's *Hamlet*, although another woman's face is singing. Here Marker introduces what looks like a solarized image. To solarize a shot you reexpose it to light, so solarizing is double exposure. We see what is happening electronically on a machine that separates the darks into lights: we see the process. This sequence recalls the editing sequence from Vertov's *The Man with the Movie Camera* (a classic nonfiction film) at the same time it begins "Krasna's" meditation on, and recollection of, a pilgrimage he made to the sites in San Francisco where Hitchcock's *Vertigo* (a classic mystery film) was shot. The fictional nonfiction filmmaker inserts footage from Hitchcock's earlier fictional movie filmed during the 1950s on location in a city (San Francisco) once almost buried under ash by earthquake and fire. One sequence or mininarrative leads by indirection into another sequence. Meanwhile the unseen narrator repairs or restores psychic reality and its relation to external reality, though we are never really certain who has collected, edited, and marked each shot or short cut.

The American-released version of *Sans Soleil* is narrated in English by Alexandra Stewart. Languages bear particular canny or uncanny acoustical patterns, historical scars. At times her narrative voiceover seems exaggerated in its accentlessness to the point where it impinges on the otherwise wonderfully varied polyphonic soundtrack. Recently I was able to see a showing of Marker's *Le Mystère Kuomiko* (1965), also filmed in Tokyo. I now notice ways in which the memory of this earlier time in Japan crops up in *Sans Soleil*, but I see the resemblance and hear the echoes belatedly. Viewers of *Vertigo*, along with Scotty (James Stewart), don't know, until three quarters of the way through the film, that Judy (Kim Novak) was impersonating Madeleine (Kim Novak). Could it be that the real Kuomiko in the cinema-verité version is a double for Hélène Chatelain (who may or may not be a professional actress), even if she doesn't speak in the ciné-roman *La Jetée*? Where is Kuomiko in the Tokyo of *Sans Soleil*? That's a later mystery. The Ginza owl is here, moving his eyes as usual, the bullet train is here, right- and left-wing radicals are here, but Kuomiko is not. The real Florence Delay is a French novelist, while "Florence Delay" could be here, editing Krasna's movie. Gavin Elster edits Madeleine's story (through Judy) in *Vertigo*. The absent cinematographer could be Delay's double except we know the unseen woman is a figment of Marker's imagination. In 1965 Kuomiko is really a young Japanese woman (perhaps a professional actress now) who speaks fluent French. Her beautiful voiceover is one of the striking elements of the Mystery that bears her name. Kim Novak's two voices as Madeleine and Judy are essential double effects in *Vertigo*. Perhaps the spoken and named voices of Delay and Stewart coappear by chance operation. My favorite sequence in *Sans Soleil* weaves in and around the Hitchcock movie. Here, the person who claims to have seen *Vertigo* nineteen times shows by subterfuge how that film's spiral of time reoccurs in *La Jetée*. So for an English-speaking viewer of *La Jetée*, *The Kuomiko Mystery*, and *Sans Soleil*, the ghostly presence of two women, their trace, is in Stewart's accentless narrative voice.

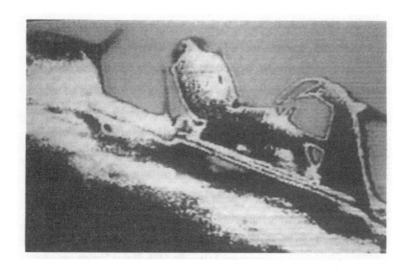

Often *Sans Soleil* seems to be largely about footage shot somewhere else. This is a film of quotations, outtakes, retakes, tape delays, failed military coups, dead pilots, and ghostly warriors. Everything is acted out on the borderline that divides introjection and incorporation. A double is a facsimile. Is *Sans Soleil's* Sandor Krasna a reflected Gavin Elster?

XVI
Film-Truth

Dziga Vertov and Chris Marker are pseudonyms.

Denis Kaufman was born in 1896 in Bialystock, then a part of the Russian Empire, now a part of Poland. His father was a bookmaker and bibliophile. I can't find information on his mother. In 1915 when he was still a child he moved with his family to Moscow. In 1917 he enrolled in the Psychoneurological Institute (special interest in human perception). The same year he organized "The Laboratory of Hearing" and experimented with sound recording. He also wrote a science-fiction novel since lost. In 1917 Kaufman abandoned his name at the threshold of his working life in film.

Christian François Bouche-Villeneuve was probably born in the Paris suburb of Neuilly-sur-Seine in 1921, possibly to a Russian mother and an American father. Other possibilities for a birthplace are Ulan Bator in Mongolia, or Belville, the Arab quarter of Paris. One bibliographic entry I found says "his early life is shrouded in mystery, much of it perpetrated by the filmmaker himself." During World War II he may have served as a resistance fighter during the occupation of France, some accounts claim he also joined the United States Army as a parachutist—he says he didn't. After the war Marker played music in bars until joining the staff of *Esprit*. He contributed poetry, political commentary, music criticism, short stories, and film essays to the influential Marxist-oriented Catholic journal. He also wrote a wartime aviation novel that has been compared to Saint-Exupéry's *Vol de Nuit* and *Pilote de Guerre*. Marker was founder, editor, and writer of the Planet series of travelogues for Editions de Seuil, which blended impressionistic journalism and still photography Marker turned to documentary filmmaking in the 1950s.

These are only some facts.

Somewhere else I read his surname may simply be a reference to magic markers, because they highlight or mark a text at the same time you can see through it.

Sans Soleil could be a rejection of the documentary form. But what about Japan, Arnilcar Cabral, and the historical context? A recent flier for a Marker retrospective at the Museum of Modern Art in New York says he discarded his baptismal name to assume the pseudonym bestowed by his friend and coworker Alain Resnais. In France a filmmaker named Christian François Bouche-Villeneuve would not be foreign, he would be French. In America a person named Chris Marker could be from any place.

The German Anschluss of Austria occurred in 1938. In 1938 Japanese and Soviet forces fought in the Far East, the Munich Conference divided up Czechoslovakia, and the Japanese announced a "New Order in East Asia." In 1938 Dziga Vertov made an entry in his notebook. "You cannot describe a house on fire until the actual event takes place. Perhaps there will be no fire. Either you'll have to deny the description as a fiction, or burn the house in accordance with the script. Then, however, it will no longer be a newsreel, but the ordinary acted film with sets and actors" (KE 217). In 1938, Bouche-Villeneuve, then seventeen, probably hadn't even thought about changing his name. Nothing is accidental. Murder is a cipher in the word "Marker."

XVII

"The first image he told me about was of three children on a road in Iceland in 1965." She remembers into the black.

The image we see is of what she says he shot or saw. It doesn't matter who is the author. The image is one of the loveliest I ever remember seeing on film. I can't say why it is so haunting, only that silence has something to do with it. Three children are moving in color but there isn't any soundtrack now. They are blonde and the sun lights their hair from behind.

Wind blowing their hair is all. The woman's hair in *La Jetée* is blown by the wind. Two of the children here are definitely girls, the other could be a boy, I'm not sure. The tallest, in the center, gives a shy, quick, furtive look towards the cameraman. All three are moving forward hand in hand, and they seem to be laughing. They could be playing a game, or they could be leading the tall one along to show her something. It's not clear who is leading who following. Just as it's not clear in *La Jetée* if the woman's smile is welcoming or warning. Silence and green fields that resemble ones I remember in Ireland. Salt air of the sea. A lyric fragment cut away. Simply peace and no evidence. They are spirits.

For Vertov, Tarkovsky, and Marker, an image introduced once as a hint or possible symbol may in another context contradict its intended leitmotif. The moment of looking is an arrest.

A minute is a minute a second front. *"One day I'll have to put it alone at the beginning of a film at the end of a long piece of black leader. If they don't see happiness at least they'll see the black leader."*

XVIII

1929. *The Man with the Movie Camera*. A dynamic tension of citizens moving forward somewhere in a large Soviet city I take to be Moscow, although it's really synthesized from Moscow, Kiev, and Odessa. The material production of life itself in a stranger stasis of silence. These trains and trolleys so flush with smoke and passengers; this young woman waking up, washing herself in her room, pulling up her stockings, fastening her bra. Silence makes it like a dream. Blinking eyes and blinking shutters. The other young woman so poor (in spite of Socialism) she has spent the night on a park bench vagrant and shy. Did physical fitness make that group of women exercising on a concrete platform happy? Did the magician juggling hoops and prestidigitating a mouse ever pass his tricks on to someone else? What are those child spectators in the audience laughing and looking at? Surely not their sure obliteration accelerated second by second. A train moves in from the background it fills the screen. Dark shapes of people then apparitions soon. Silent recesses as if they haven't been leveled already by hard usage by coordinating retrospect.

If a trace is the insertion of words in time, this time what *is* is the wordless acceleration of formal development combined with buoyant enthusiasm.

Disaster is coming; they can't see nor know what we know now.

1982. Dziga Vertov's *The Man with the Movie Camera* is iconoclastic, revolutionary, tectonic, alert. Chris Marker is a man with a movie camera traveling in the wake of World War II. In *Sans Soleil* we sense the failure of revolutionary enthusiasm. "Poetry is born of insecurity," says Marker's voiceover persona, referring to the Japanese habit of living for appearance.

XIX

The off-screen person speaking and writing through her voice. Three children holding hands. A woman's hand touching the railing of a ferry. Other fragments of sound without words through thought mirror the military instructor's beating heart without having to translate an author's creative stockpile from past to present. "I'm just back from Hokkaido, the northern island." Now we know he means Japan. Passengers are sleeping on the benches of the ferry. Shots of their arms thrown over their faces in sleep. They could be dead and wounded. Sight of so many sleeping so randomly drifting. He thinks *"of a past or future war. Night trains air raids fallout shelters."*

The title of *Sans Soleil* comes after the first three images. The next is of a foghorn on the side of a ferry going somewhere. It is almost sunless. No narration. The sound of the ship's engine resembles the noise of a heart beating. A heart is an engine. When your heart stops there is nothing. No color no sun no sound no time. The entrance of the Ghost in Olivier's *Hamlet* is marked by a heartbeat sound effect suggesting a drumbeat. Now as then it's dawn. We see a shot of a woman's hand resting on the rail of the ferry. She has a watch on her wrist, her other hand touches the railing lightly. She appears to be talking to someone and turns in his direction. The direction is the same one the ship is moving in, toward the right-hand frame of the film. The children of the introduction were walking the opposite way.

Something at the margin between thought and sound is somewhere else. The message arrives as a departure. All thoughts are winged. *La Jetée* forms a sound within sound that is other than jetty. *Sans Soleil* says one thing, "Sunless" means the same but not exactly.

So many hyphens and parentheses surround him.

That road and that place. Restructuring quickening joy to light through editing until destiny reverses division. Human beauty and human clarity carry the Force of a reproach. Short cut and black leader. Military aircraft under the deck of a destroyer. Ethics or aesthetic contrast. Writing is a cutting from inside to paper. Nonfiction footage conveys the world outside. Military background imagery. Too bad for the children.
Another nonfiction attempt at realism.

Ophelia: They say the owl was a baker's daughter. Lord, we know what we are, but know not what we may be.

All people captured on film are ghosts. They appear and do not appear. "Be thou, Spirit fierce, / My spirit! Be thou me, impetuous one! / Drive my dead thoughts over the universe" Shelley wrote in "Ode to the West Wind," Emerson, in the essay called "Language," says we are like travelers using the cinders of a volcano to roast their eggs. The woman is reading Marker's written multiple-changeover commentary with practiced utterance. Words are the symbols of spirits. The deer and the dear run away.

After the Third War was there resistance? What happens in current revolutionary institutions when films and tapes rot?

Ivan has gone to reconnoiter in the "dead, flooded forest." Mother of dreams come cover your son's staring photograph.

invisible colliding phenomena.

I entered crazily into the spectacle into the image taking in my arms what i
ing to die as Nietzsche did when on January 23, 1889
anagram and each splitting element
I entered crazily into the spectacle into the image taking in my arms what is i:
going to die as Nietzsche did when on January 23, 1889
The obscurity of what I felt you felt
There may be a number of messages in
There may be a number of messages in
I entered crazily into the spectacle into the image taking in my arms what
going to die as Nietzsche did when on January 23, 1889
painting. Nevertheless, I love the view
The obscurity of what I felt you felt

The reality of chance. A choice of masks. Political leadership wasn't always an appropriate focus for analysis. Amilcar Cabral approached life dialectically. In his absence he is far from clear. There is a vast literature even during the armed phase.

The poverty of reality in a world market. Viewpoint web-camera equipment.

Editing historical necessity at a periphery.

Blank the crack and mark no language or predator camera can recover.

Remember.

1994. *Facsimile*

The village of Pavlovskoe near Moscow. A screening. The small place is filled with peasant men and women and workers from a nearby factory. *Kinopravda* is being shown, without musical accompaniment. The noise of the projector can be heard. On the screen a train speeds past. A young girl appears, walking straight toward the camera. Suddenly a scream is heard in the hall. A woman runs toward the girl on the screen. She's weeping, with her arms stretched out before her. She calls the girl by name. But the girl disappears. On the screen the train rushes by once more. The lights are turned on in the hall. The woman is carried out unconscious. "What's going on?" a worker-correspondent asks. One of the viewers answers: "It's kino-eye. They filmed the girl while she was still alive. Not long ago she fell ill and died. The woman running toward the screen was her mother"
—Dziga Vertov (KE 85).

Refused mourning or melancholia here is the camera the film the projector.